Y0-EIA-751

CHICAGO PUBLIC LIBRARY
HUMBOLDT PARK BRANCH
1605 N. TROY STREET
CHICAGO, IL 60647
(312) 744-2244

Yellow Umbrella Books are published by Red Brick Learning
7825 Telegraph Road, Bloomington, Minnesota 55438
http://www.redbricklearning.com

Library of Congress Cataloging-in-Publication Data
Ring, Susan.
    [Taking care of pets. Spanish]
    Cuidando a las mascotas/por Susan Ring.
    p. cm.
    ISBN-13: 978-0-7368-6006-2 (hardcover)
    ISBN-10: 0-7368-6006-1 (hardcover)
    ISBN 0-7368-3074-X (softcover)
    1. Pets—Juvenile literature. I. Title.
SF416.2.R5717 2006
636.088'7—dc22   2005054303

Written by Susan Ring
Developed by Raindrop Publishing

Editorial Director: Mary Lindeen
Editor: Jennifer VanVoorst
Photo Researcher: Wanda Winch
Adapted Translations: Gloria Ramos
Spanish Language Consultants: Jesús Cervantes, Anita Constantino
Conversion Assistants: Jenny Marks, Laura Manthe

Copyright © 2006 Red Brick Learning. All rights reserved.
No part of this book may be reproduced without written permission from
the publisher. The publisher takes no responsibility for the use of any of
the materials or methods described in this book, nor for the products thereof.
Printed in the United States of America.

Photo Credits
Cover: SW Productions/PhotoDisc; Title Page: Ryan McVay/PhotoDisc;
Page 4: Hoa Qui/Index Stock; Page 6: Gary Sundermeyer/Capstone Press;
Page 8: Nicole Katano/Brand X Pictures; Page 10: Gary Sundermeyer/Capstone Press;
Page 12: Gary Sundermeyer/Capstone Press; Page 14: Gary Sundermeyer/Capstone
Press; Page 16: Image Source/elektraVision

1 2 3 4 5 6 11 10 09 08 07 06

Cuidando a las mascotas

por Susan Ring

JUV/E Sp SF 416.2 .R5718
Ring, Susan.
Cuidando a las mascotas

Yellow Umbrella Books
for early readers

R03230 28614
HUMBOLDT PARK

Mi amiga cuida
a su mascota.

Mi amigo cuida
a su mascota.

Mi amiga cuida
a su mascota.

Mi amigo cuida
a su mascota.

Mi amiga cuida
a su mascota.

Mi amigo cuida
a su mascota.

Yo cuido
a mi mascota.

Índice

amiga, 5, 9, 13
amigo, 7, 11, 15

cuida, 5, 7, 9, 11, 13, 15
mascota, 5, 7, 9, 11, 13, 15, 17